Windm

MW01092870

Coloring Book For Adults

Collection of Dutch Mills & Windmill Landscapes - Hand Drawn Sketches

Rachel Mintz

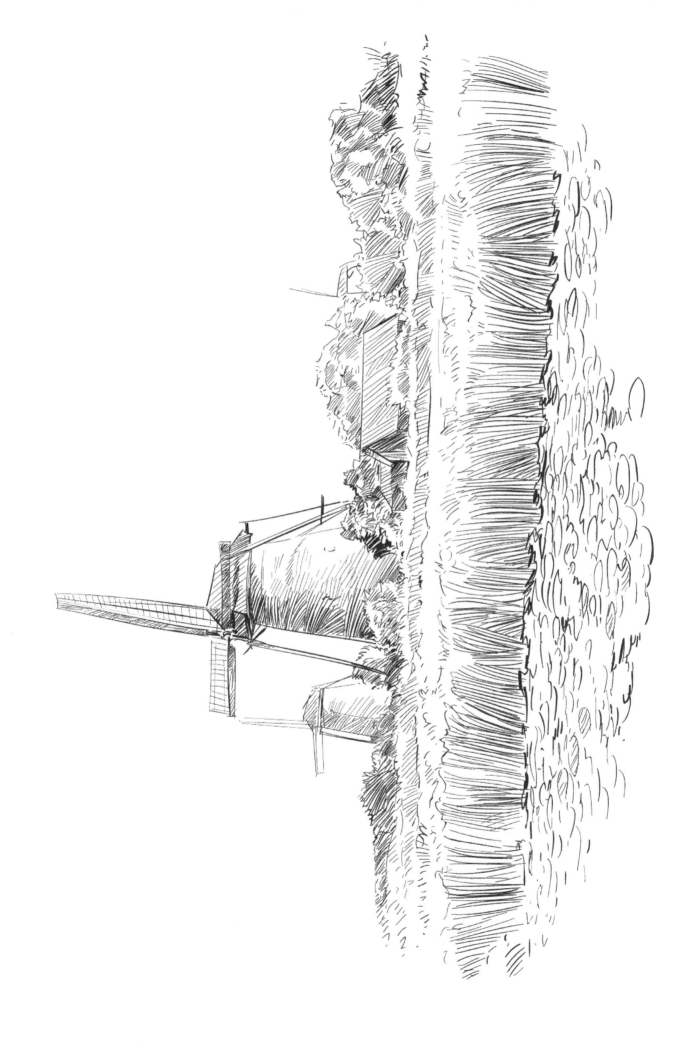

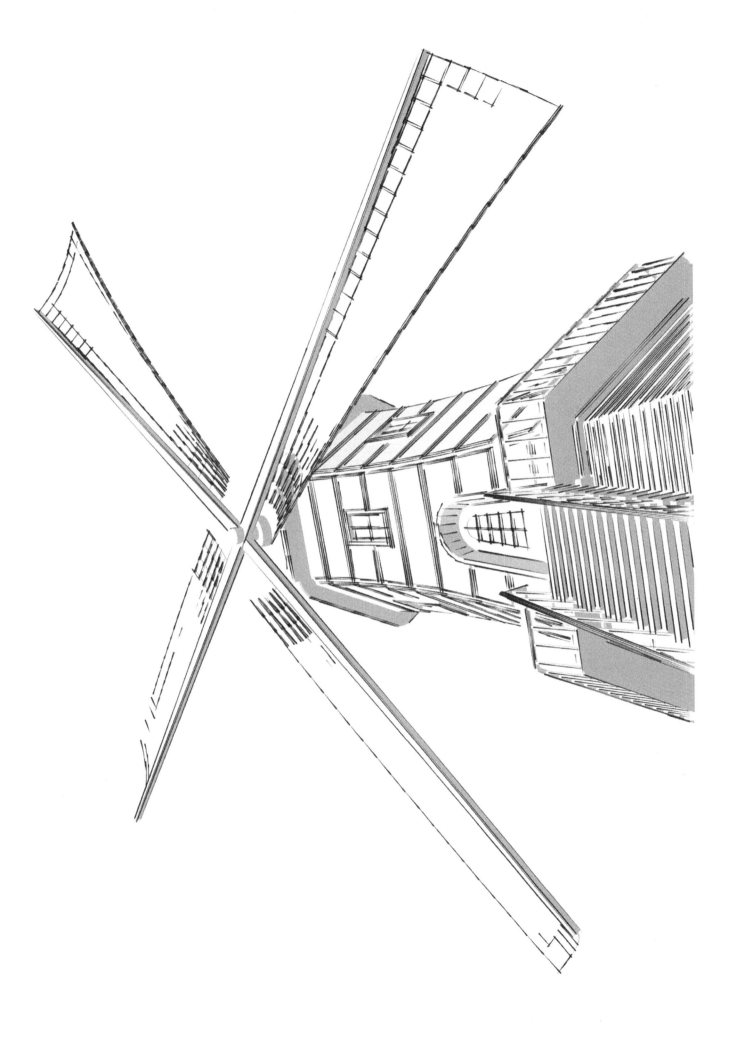

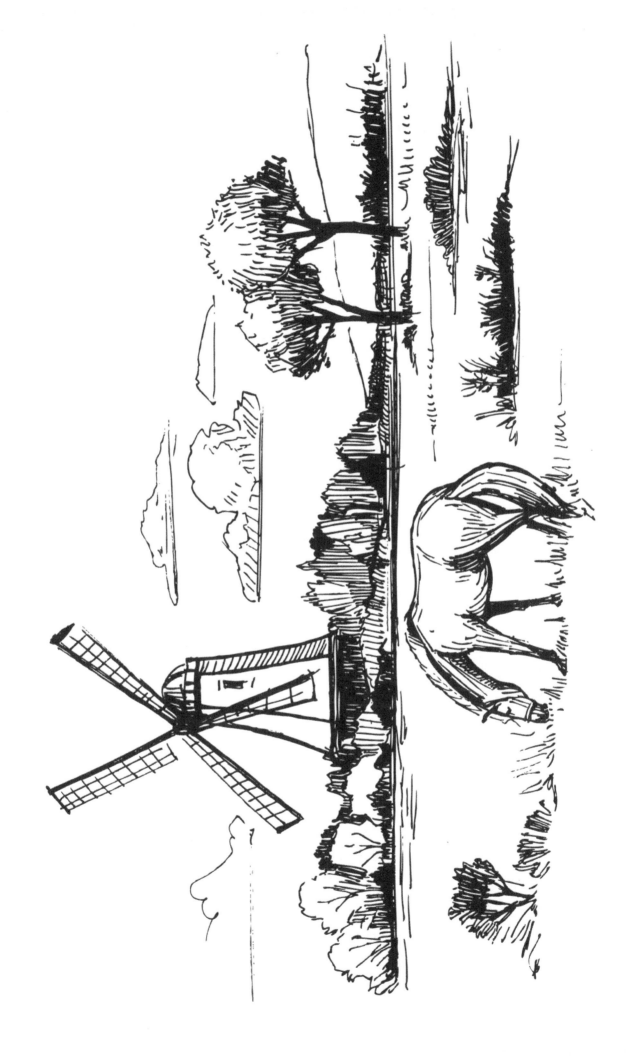

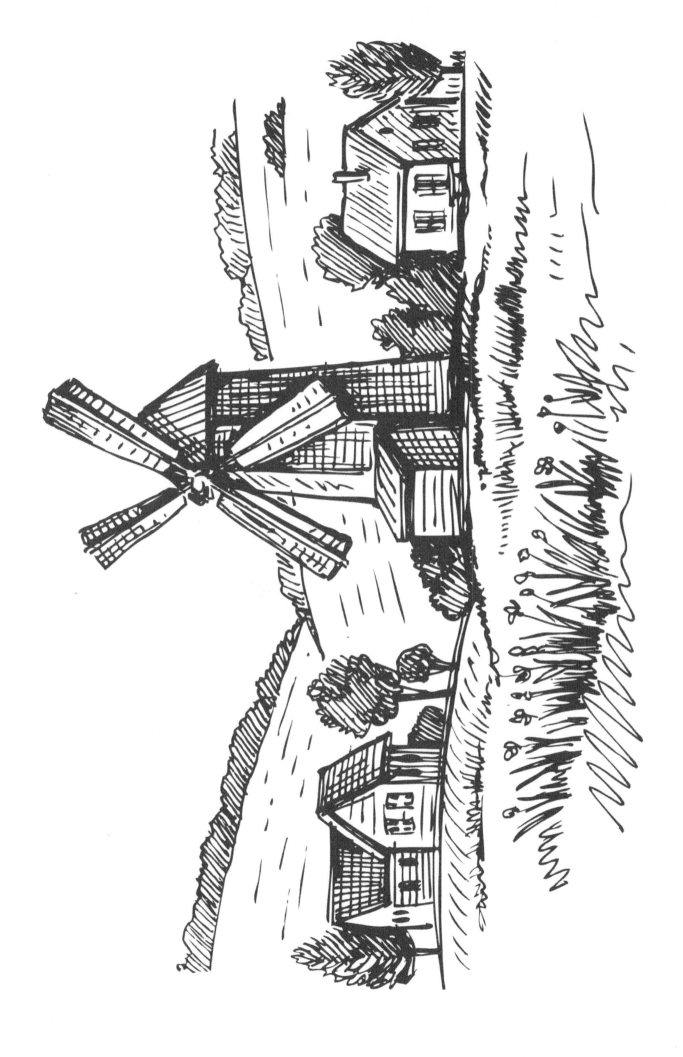

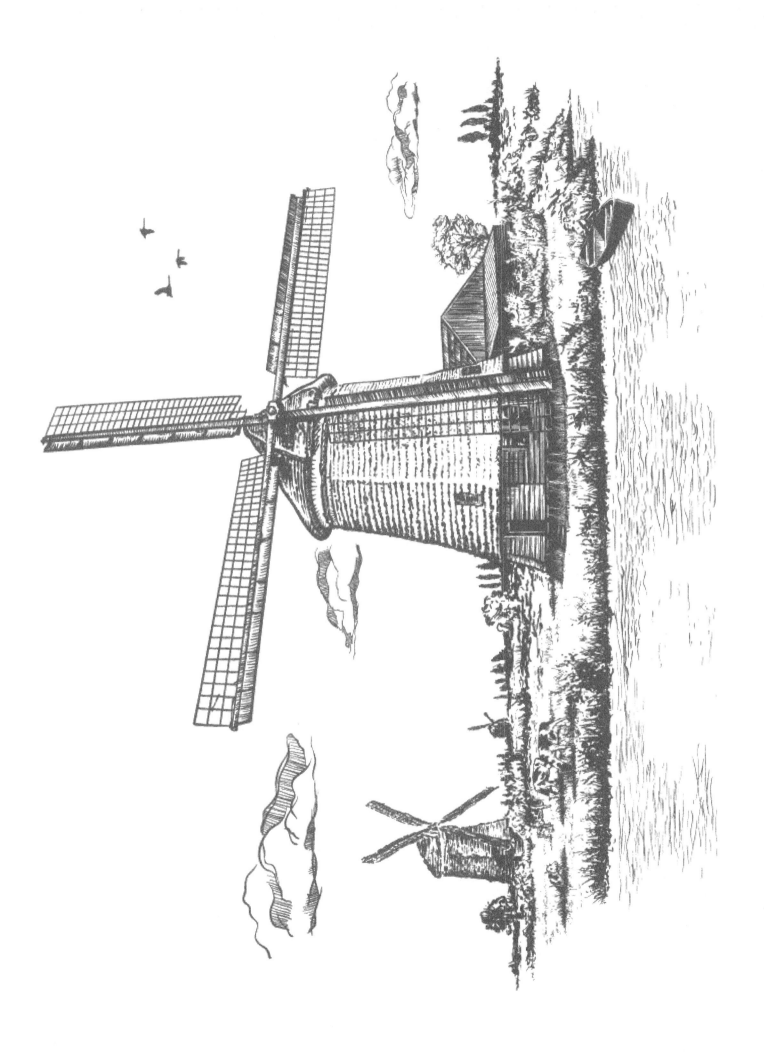

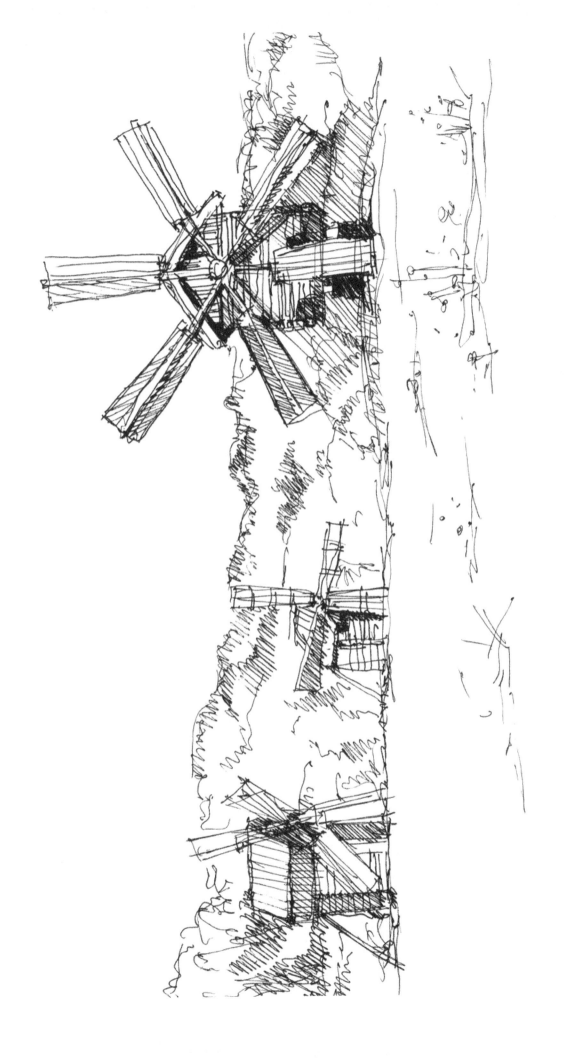

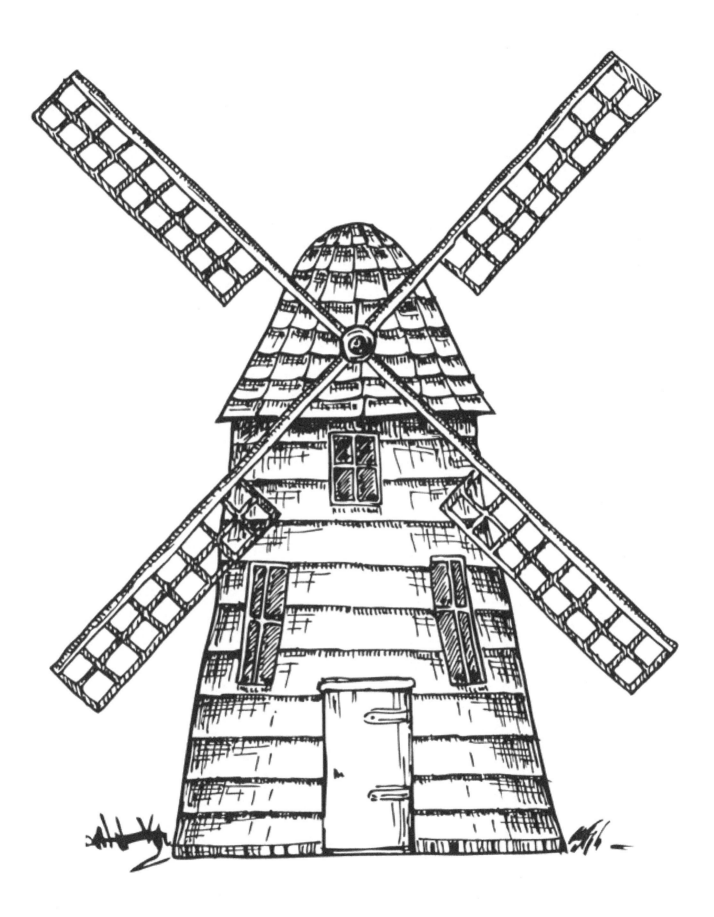

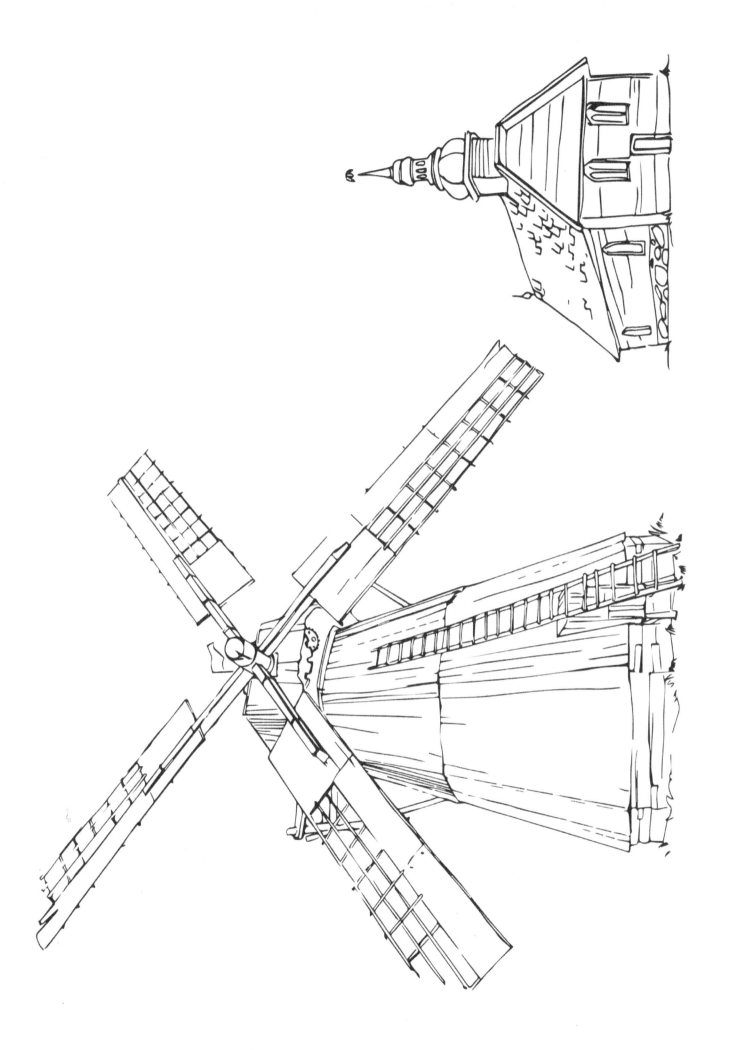

Thank you for coloring with us

Enjoy more from our coloring books catalog:

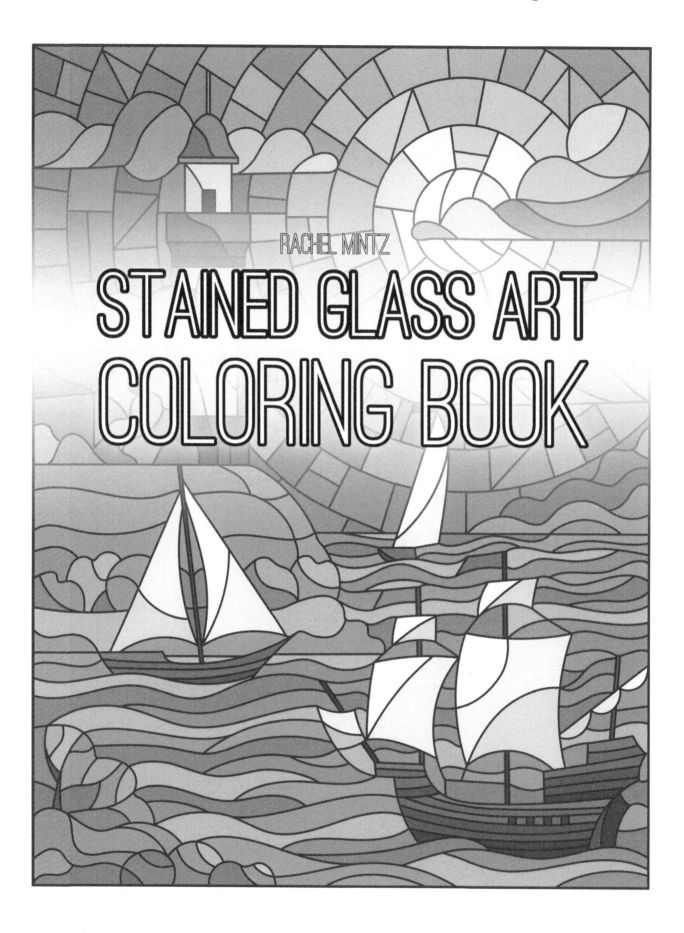

LUXURY BEDROOMS

COLORING BOOK FOR ADULTS

RACHEL MINTZ

THE BEAUTY OF
PRAGUE
COLORING BOOK

RACHEL MINTZ

BEAUTIFUL LIGHTHOUSES
COLORING BOOK

RACHEL MINTZ

Thank you for coloring with us.

Made in the USA
Middletown, DE
10 June 2022